THE HOLY RANGER: HARLEY-DAVIDSON POEMS
MARTIN JACK ROSENBLUM

RANGER INTERNATIONAL PRODUCTIONS
LION PUBLISHING/ROAR RECORDING
MILWAUKEE
1989

Some of the poems in this text appear revised from the limited edition chapbook, *Harley-Davidson Poems*, and none can be reproduced in any form or by any means, electronic or mechanical, including photocopying and recording, or by any information storage and retrieval systems, without written permission from the author - exceptions are brief passages quoted in newspaper, magazine, radio or television reviews. All rights reserved. First Edition, August, 1989.

Typesetting by Membrane Press. Luis Machare, front cover illustration; John Mallow, back cover photograph; Design Group, Inc., cover design. Willie G. Davidson, Vice-President of Styling at Harley-Davidson, Cover Forward.

Since little is closer to the heart of a Harley owner than a natural American landscape, this book has been printed on 100% recycled paper; and like a Harley, this book was made in the U.S.A.

Copyright © 1989 by Martin Jack Rosenblum.

Library of Congress Catalog Card Number: 89-083936

Softcover Trade Edition: 089018-053-9
Hardcover Gift Edition: 089018-054-7

Ranger International Productions
Lion Publishing/Roar Recording
Post Office Box 71231
Milwaukee
Wisconsin 53211-7331

Author's Note to the First Edition

The author extends appreciation to many Harley-Davidson representatives, from executive offices to dealerships, who supported this project through practical considerations and inspirational comradery. Quoting from the author's "mailbag" letter in the fall, 1988 *Enthusiast* will explain further: "As a Harley owner, I am proud to be part of the organization that goes to such caring and detailed lengths to make riding a Harley-Davidson so much more than just being on a motorcycle -- when one rides a Harley, one sits on top of an important tradition that transcends the machine itself. One steers a certain American spirit into personal territory." *Harley-Davidson Poems* is this personal territory, then, steered into through the poetic process of Harley ownership, riding and fraternal zeal.

This book is dedicated to Sarah Terez and Molly Dvora, little girls who would not consider themselves to be properly dressed unless they are showing Harley emblems, and to Maureen, whose willingness to have a Sportster next to the dinner table in winter has got to be an expression of true love for the author.

Author's Preface to the Present Edition

The first edition of my Harley poetry was limited and less ambitious, but was given trademark approval by Tom Parsons, Trademark Manager, Harley-Davidson, Inc., who was as moved as I was to witness *Harley-Davidson Poems* sell out in a matter of months following its release in December, 1988. There was a book release party at Jerry Renner's House of Harley-Davidson, sponsored by the Milwaukee Chapter of Harley Owners Group that month, and the attendance defied all expectations. Tom was then instrumental in making *The Holy Ranger: Harley-Davidson Poems* an Official Licensed Product and he has my gratitude, as does Judge Robert Schneider who provided the material spark to keep the visionary flame lit; my appreciation also goes to my loving family again for putting up with my eccentric ways and sometimes overbearing inspirations. I have always known what I must do, and admit to doing it with an intensity that gets the job done: without the understanding of my wife and daughters, I would not be writing as forcefully as I now am.

> *We are men and we have words.*
> Paul Blackburn

Introduction to the First Edition
Joel McNally
The Milwaukee Journal

Martin J. Rosenblum describes his limited edition Harley-Davidson Sportster as the ideal urban steed. He rides it into an American past populated with Texas Rangers and mountain men and political outlaws.

Rosenblum did not fulfill his childhood dream of owning a Harley until he was entering his forties. By that time, he had established himself among an international community of artists known as the Objectivist Poets and earned a doctoral degree as a scholar in this field. He had undergone a career change. He quit trying to teach poetry at the university level to take a job that he considered of more use to his community, advising students who lacked college skills. He was recovering from a near-fatal illness.

"I realized that it was time to do the things I wanted to do. One of these was to own a perfect specimen of a Harley."

He had it delivered on a snowy, mid-winter day even though it would be months before he would be able to ride it. Rosenblum remembers going through an ordinary workday filled with joy at the incredible notion: "I've got a Harley-Davidson in my living room." Late that night, he got up and went downstairs alone. The only lights he turned on were the lights of the bike. He sat next to it in a chair for a long time.

"It's a subject of curiosity on both sides that I'm this intellectual poet-philosopher who wears leathers. But, on the Harley side, I'm more understood than on the university side. They know why I love Harleys."

A student of American history, Rosenblum collects what he considers the essence of American products in areas he has practical expertise -- Colt pistols, Gibson guitars and, now, a Harley-Davidson. He identifies Harley with the rugged individualists of the past. He sees no reason why bikers should be considered criminally inclined. "The image of a Harley owner as some kind of degenerate is false

The Holy Ranger Poems / v

just as the image of an artist as a degenerate is false. Both can be healthy lifestyles. Owning a Harley has something to do with an archetypal sense of the frontier, just as being an artist does but there the frontier is more internal. Riding a Harley motorcycle is a spiritual feeling of being out on the range, and my *Harley-Davidson Poems* is the result."

Although he has no love for Japanese motorcycles, he compares Harley-Davidson riding to Eastern meditation and the discipline he has pursued for years in martial arts.

"Each time I get on, I quiet myself. I have no other purpose. I'm not running an errand. I don't use this bike to go to work. When I'm on my Sportster, I'm really riding it. It's like the oriental tea ceremony. When you pour the tea, you're really pouring it and you don't spill a drop. This is my understanding of what meditation is. I probably pray more in a twenty-four hour period than most holy men do. I just do it on a Harley."

Re: Marty Rosenblum, The Holy Ranger
From: Buzz Buzzelli, "Enthusiast" Editor
To: Readers of this Harley Poetry

Poetry? About Riding Harleys?

I'm sure! And how about using humming birds to power freight trains? After all, poetry (you know, that boring i * am * bic * pen * ta * meter stuff that reads like plagiarized hillbilly song lyrics) can't possibly communicate the feeling of riding, right?

Then I met Marty . . . Okay, so I was wrong.

People who ride Harley-Davidson motorcycles understand that motorcycling is a unique, individual experience. It can mean many things to different people: the sensation of motion, the sensual feeling of the wind, the reflection on other thoughts and feelings or simply enjoying a comradery with others who also enjoy riding, to name a few. A rider may feel one of these, or all, and more, from one moment to another.

Like the fluid experience of riding, Marty's poetic rustle through the mind triggers unique reactions that result from each rider's individual experience. This isn't just about riding; it's about life surrounded by Harleys, about a motorcycling lifestyle.

Marty's poetry and riding Harleys? A natural combination!

Introduction to The Holy Ranger: Harley-Davidson Poems
Howard McCord, Professor of English Literature

The Holy Ranger is a pure crystal in the complex solution of contemporary American mythopoetics. Martin Jack Rosenblum has achieved this concentration of clarity and intensity by living through language the fusion of the many versions of the American hero, his steed, and his quest for freedom. The Holy Ranger is not only the rider, but his Harley-Davidson as well, his single-action Colt, and the wild roar of the wind as he rides into pure, timeless actuality.

Martin Jack Rosenblum is a poet who has dipped into the archetypal reservoirs of our culture for themes and images which possess great energy and he has articulated them with precision into richly original language alive with music, idea, and emotion. His poems carry the reader into the wilderness of perfect perception, into moments when act and will and being are fused and whole. In "The Heart Must Beat In An Accurate Hand," he speaks of "objects in absolute/need of control, " which describes the poem as succinctly as it describes our hearts, and the difficulty of bringing either to conformity with an ideal is the process of our lives. The Holy Ranger must exercise control over his Sportster and the Colt in his hand, as well as his line-breaks and images, if he is to live free in mastery of himself. The sense of freedom Martin Jack Rosenblum creates and celebrates is a reflection of the mastery and control he possesses as an artist.

Parallel with ideals of mental discipline and intensity are their social counterparts: loyalty, honesty, chivalry, trust, and the responsibility for self-reliance. The social order proposed is profoundly American. The armed freeholder who is quick to defend himself and the common good, and determined to preserve his own independence, provide his own livelihood, and to preserve the peace with diligence is the ideal citizen in the eyes of the framers of the Constitution. The dilution and corruption of this ideal by a political ideology that proposes that the government knows best how its citizens should live, and legislation which limits individual freedoms and responsibilities by creating greater dependency on government alms is cause for righteous anger and wrath in the Holy Ranger.

"The Holy Ranger As Avenging Angel" is a central poem in the collection which examines and mourns the losses of liberty suffered under a paternalistic, cosseting government, and in a social order corrupted by the lies and distortions of the press and television, the wheedling, vapid mouthings of politicians, clergy, and money-grubbers, and the machinations of a judicial system less interested in punishing criminals than in protecting their "rights." It is clear that in a society both drifting and being driven into decadence, it is imperative that the Holy Ranger obey such a dictum as Whitman's "resist much, obey little."

But if the Holy Ranger is an idealist, he is also a sensualist, an artist as appreciative of elegant form and function in motorcycle and firearm as he is of beauty and passion in a woman. That Americans are not supposedly capable of sophisticated sensuality is a canard of French critics and their ilk (who can legitimately be accused of most sins most of the time), and dour souls soured by the bad breath of Puritanism. Such forget the Puritans were as they were because they were so randy.

It is no great leap of imagination to see Tom Jefferson astride a Harley, roaring down the paths of Monticello in full delight, or know with what passionate interest Ben Franklin might have carefully disassembled one of Samuel Colt's or John Browning's pistols. We are a nation of practical sensualists, Frenchmen, and don't you forget it!

Martin Jack Rosenblum is uniquely aware among poets of the way technology has shaped our consciousness, and entered the myth of our vision of ourselves. Whitman understood the psychic power of the locomotives which were linking and binding the several States into unity. Rosenblum understands how individualized technology -- as the motorcycle and the pistol are designed to be controlled

The Holy Ranger Poems / ix

by one will only -- preserve and strengthen the individual in an age of homogenization and reduction.

It is with the spare and direct language so characteristic of the Objectivist poets that Martin Jack Rosenblum shapes his poetry. The Objectivists form a proud lineage in American poetry of the twentieth century, getting their impetus from Pound and Williams, and numbering such great poets as Louis Zukofsky, George Oppen, Lorine Niedecker, Basil Bunting, Carl Rakosi, Charles Reznikoff, Cid Corman, Carl Thayler, and Theodore Enslin among them. Each of these has a distinctive voice and presence certainly, but they share much also:plain speech, hard thinking, precise conceptualization, and rich musicality. Martin Jack Rosenblum is a worthy younger member of this important group of American poets, and in *The Holy Ranger: Harley-Davidson Poems* he has added a significant volume to that canon.

Now turn the page. Ride. Live free.

FIRST SEQUENCE: ESSENTIALS

No, don't nod.
Look me square in the face:
see the glittering in my eyes.

Karl Young

The First Look

The Holy Ranger returned from that ride, begun at sunrise much earlier this day, with sidepipes rumbling in the rhythm of twin cylinders beating an American pulse. He dismounted, and before going into Holy Ranger Headquarters, considered just how to relate the adventures of the road to those who understand what it can mean. Poetry was a suitable medium, he realized, for he knew it well by now and recognized that it was as close to the rhythm of the iron mount he rode as any form of communication might be.

He had a dream last night about historical identities -- people who have influenced the course of American life. The Holy Ranger believes that it is the individual who should be studied, not the times or events; it is the brave, solitary person who is responsible for all that makes an era or incident take on meaning for others to share.

Before going to sleep, he had been taking the first look at an old photograph of the men whose names have literally become motorcycle reality: he watched as one inventive genius, standing there next to his Harley-Davidson, among the others who have also become cultural eponyms, and who are --like us all-- on the ride, suddenly roared from black and white truth to full color vision in front of the original shack where real motorcycles were first bred in Milwaukee.

It is by this route, then, that poetry is created regarding the Harley experience, and the Holy Ranger will call it *EvoPoetics*: common occurrence comes into its intrinsic nature through an evolutionary process of visionary content. The engine that is now an evolution wonder itself has pounded a poetic meter into the lives of many rugged individualists, and this book is written to celebrate all that handling American Iron horsepower maneuvers into The Holy Ranger's fountain pen.

He does not use word-processing, for computers do not function when the power goes out. The Holy Ranger is prepared for the failures of modern civilization, and rides in search of the Old American Way with an understanding that an advance has to mean a hard look back. There are people behind us from whom present lessons must be learned, and people now, too, whom we must judge by virtue of their knowledge of the past as they bring us into future possibility. The Holy Ranger writes his poetry as a tribute to these pioneers, past and present, who cut the trail into a more promising American Way of life. These are the horsemen who are on an apocalyptic ride.

The Holy Ranger is blessed and humbled to know some of them, and intends to celebrate their individuality and style, for there is no greater contribution he can make to a nation that still is being carved out of territories unknown by riders who can righteously handle where they journey.

The Name Is Harley

standing there with the look
of invention in front of that
original shack new ideas took
hold which built a reputation
all the way into the American ideas

that govern individuality & style   :
William S. Harley has lent his name

to the modern horsemen whose
apocalyptic   ride   strengthens
open   trail   visions   that   make

this photographic action take place
this sunrise in April as I take the
keys to my Harley machine then walk

the irregular stone path to
the garage contemplating in
poetic anticipation   exactly
what   will
be coming
within   an
afternoon -
upon   this
Iron Name

.

Two Meditations Upon an XLH 1100 Sportster

1.
the view from behind
these buckhorns down
      Hiway Q with
      peanut tank
in sun & this V-Twin
a pounding metaphor:
distant birds single
file along meadows &
   the downshift into
   second gear brings
   flight nearer road
     speed when my

Harley-Davidson cracks
the envelope of visionary carburation.
2.
standing on the footpegs in Wisconsin:
nearer dusk then
easing back into

saddle posture away
from plains with a twitch
in the right wrist sending
a message out from shorty duals
that arriving has occurred just by
starting this Sunday morning when a
pleasing vibration was sent through
chrome headers to assure a dominant

pioneer strength even from
an urban Milwaukee range   .

The Holy Ranger Poems / 5

**Talking with Willie G.
at the Harley Homecoming Ride Celebration**

now here's a guy who
likes to ride which is
what happens when you talk

with him
suddenly

that sense of steel-tipped
boot up on the shifter gets
into sentences through the gears

.

Harley-Davidson Is In Milwaukee

the Monday James Marsh called
from England I was delayed from
my university office having spent
time with the 1989 Harley Accessory
Catalog in the bathroom after Wisconsin
cheese melted on a whole wheat muffin made
in Milwaukee County caused the body to stir

not unpleasantly for admiring the possibility of
a windshield on "Ranger" takes requisite pushing

of imagination as a Sporty with one never stirred
sensibility nor impulse until this winter's eye
injury still fresh now on the first day of
spring we have March snow & the fireplace
stoked but I put the battery right off
a trickle-charger into the bike still
tucked into its vinyl eagle nest
(sloshing through the ice to
the garage the stone curved
path a slippery uncut
trail we're used to
with winter growling nearly as loud
         as the V-Twin melting
       rumble that announces spring
     in Milwaukee better than any frightened
bulb shipped in from the East Coast unable
to poke through ground frost will   )

 so a call from the BBC got me into a DC-9
saddle cutting this air trail to the Harley-

Davidson Museum stuck in York Pennsylvania
& from my first seat row I rode backwards:

The Holy Ranger Poems / 7

which is appropriate
because I can keep my eye
on Juneau Avenue & Capitol Drive
original facilities in Milwaukee
Wisconsin with my back
to Pensylvania's
Milwaukee Iron   .

Midwestern Handling

for Jack Grassel,
Dear Friend

    next door there's
one of those Jap bikes with
the cowl painted to give an
international racing scream
to the rider sitting behind
fiberglass that gets colder
than leathers   .

    up my front walk
an ancient Harley-Davidson
Sportster is ridden this
Sunday & into my house
a dear friend & his
son bring along the
fast temperature drop
that has sucked early spring
back into winter's exhaust .
when he leaves his little
boy hangs onto this
mastodon from hell
& those sidepipes
burn leftover leaves
that are not ready now for
         summer's rake

         .

nor does that red, white
& blue cabaret racer with
its anodized pipes start
as an owner pushes it
toward a garage the
only smoke from
his breathing here in

The Holy Ranger Poems / 9

      Milwaukee where cold
      hangs onto you as
      the roar of bright
      chrome headers while
your friend tears down
hardening gutter water
blowing heaven's grace
further into Midwestern hands

·

Evolution Amulet

the 30th Anniversary XLH sat in the diningroom
during winter months & once after a late movie
when all slept & the first real snow landed
I got on it & turned the lights toward a
front window shining into the blanket
being tossed upon the birch tree
as winter's comfort & signaling
with yellow flashes reflecting
on an empty television screen:
the first spring rain bringing
this Sportster down the ramp
& across the lawn & sidewalk
to the garage where it
fires up once the carb
swallows ample passion
but the rain keeps any
travel in the alley to
 just beads upon fresh
wax or upon the chrome my reflection
while I get down nearer the exhausts
to hear what winter kept in silence.

Praise Our Ladies

these Harley women
straddle their choppers
with lustrous precision
& when packing behind you
with hands tucked under the
belt buckle at your waist a
man rides amidst powers of
awesome potential & the
bike actually lathers
like a stallion
bulging at that
barndoor   .

Ranger Visionary

when I was not a teenager the Harley newsletters
would come by subscription even though my father
did not permit any talk of motorcycles
& the photos in these of those Highway
Patrol riders remind me now
      not a teenager either : of the
                 sofa I called
      my mount when I would either
      ride a horse as a Texas Ranger
      or a cycle but on both there were
      my chaps & holsters & with cap guns
      blazing the living room would contain
dead bad guys especially when I pulled the lever
-action from the scabbard   ·
father had been in the Swedish Palace Guard Corps
& then a marksman in the U.S. Army but no members
of his household could talk of motorcycles beyond
finding them as he did once in a sidecar that was
driven by a drunken Swede through Norwegian roads
      so I collected those newsletters that
      started in elementary school fantasy.
hell, now I
have the chaps
once again & while
I can't holster my Colt
Peacemakers in Wisconsin
I sure have nice saddlebags
slung over the back fender for
them and no scabbard but that Winchester
might knock against either horn or carburator
as I dig my still imaginary spurs (as these would
certainly be unnecessary with forty-five degrees
worth of horses to throttle) into "Ranger" -- close
enough to the name I had for that old green sofa
in my father's house to keep being grown-up more
useful than it would be if I wasted child's play

                  ·

The Holy Ranger Poems / 13

Balance
(Required Off Motorcycle)

I.

our dog wanders
in a circle tracing
on the kitchen floor
before settling down .
            this does not
    do much but cause
  her dismay as she

bumps into our
daughter on the
floor as well staking
out territory for toys   .

Sarah Terez moves over the surface
with a stuffed reindeer which might
be a moose heading for the dollhouse
where assorted rubber people watch the
dog finally flop down on a bracelet & two
rings . Sarah pats Marta
       now old & white muzzle draped with
       silk scarves as she is part of the
       game to deserve space this Sunday
          on the head as if
          to congratulate
          for making it
          a safe place
          in this wild
          place & then   kicks her nose playing
                            with a truck . the leaves

begin to fall
there is colder

air along floorboards
& earlier against the
sharp sky geese flew
honking   stirrings
            belonging
to divided years my
garden finally felt
its first frost
last night & my

ability to listen to a new
recording master of untamed
music made before last night
an instrumental version   is altered
                          by visions
of beasts nearing a family dwelling   &
I am wandering at the edges of our
housed autumn in dismay   .

II.

I open a window
& let weighted air
in or out : I do not
know which will help

            .

III.

I come up after the hall
light went back on so she
could sleep she said   &
entered our own room   &
                was a

witness to the lady
on the corner turning
on her overhead bulb that got
     spliced by
    blinds into light
    edges contoured

  by your hips
  in the dark
  they went
  onto the   carpet arranged

by a dog breathing now in hot
weather & I patted her onto me
they came & when I got to where
they rose & fell or your long legs
did by morning another bright source
through blind slats less artificial but
the familiar impact of entering this
southeast division etched relative
to neighborhood & planetary
resources placing something
    over my eyes as I get up
           with which
  to see
  I look   at your sleep
          falling up the
pillow against shelf items away
from a bed I will be in again &
     again with you traced

.

IV.

a different dog now
since I watched Marta
go with shoulders down
in compliance to surgery
& death this one pedigreed
quite willing to slaughter
those unwelcome to a
widening circle but
within narrowing
grace   :
clamping   a blueprint
              to scale my
arms resting on a sticky
maple table as the Waterman
nears the end of its reservoir
              & I would get
more ink but there is no
emergency path cut from
kitchen to study   .

V.

there is another child
now pulsing in Maureen
so I will just watch   .

VI.

                    before I
           am out in
           Downer's Woods ample
Canadian Geese in unison their
clock feathers
mark earth fog
none wanders   .

VII.

once in the Northern Wisconsin

forests I heard the Loon
in morning fog
a   ghost flight
to the water & its sound

a genuine dismay over the firelanes, not mine

                                      .

Motorcycle Noon

with the sun straight as the road
                        there is a wind tattoo
upon my bare hands designed by which route I
have taken
    through Milwaukee County farmland where
a Soo Line freight will pass on the track
side of me & on the field's edge to the
other a John Deere tractor pulls a
spreader in a turn : all reflection in pond
                        water is still & ahead
full reverie in tire hum inks raw prayer to
motorcycle designs that respond
                to clutch upon religious shifts.

EvoPoetics: Harley Poetry Mechanics

the toolbox has been spilled
onto the office floor behind
the garage & there are books
with wrenches thrown in them
for poetic meter is valuable

when it chugs inside
a process evolved
up from literary
origins down
roads upon
which chunks from an

old wooden bridge foundation
laid over with blacktop will

protrude in the worn spots
& present dangerous travel
that no book tells you how
to avoid & the wrench then
with instinct replaces any
mechanical study: the ride

will take you
where it goes   .

Holy Ranger Vision Territory

along 5 Mile Road off Interstate 94
The Holy Ranger met up with that
lost rider often heard on
Wisconsin back routes
rumbling near gravel
shoulders on an Iron Redskin at the
                         edge of summer
just before the heat rises from day
clear into evening's ground gully fog

                         .

the year had been 1846 & this
ghost rider was among the Texas Ranger
bunch riding victoriously to secure US
borders & when in the following year
the advancing horsemen lost their
commander fresh from meeting Samuel
Colt who put a brace of Walker pistols
in this brave leader's leather gunbelt
         this man went down with
            Captain Walker a musket round
                     into each(from
that saddle then he fell into summer's
early Wisconsin rural roads where once
into Holy Ranger Territory he dismounted

                         .

"poetry rides the wind
we prowl" the old gent
said: with history's
       footpegs under
his boots to balance
against headwind The
Holy Ranger along an open Heartland
                    cement trail
         snapped handgrip reins
& saluted this phantom patriot who
survived to ride upon one summer's
edge in sacred territorial vision.

The Holy Ranger Poems / 21

Early Spring on a Harley-Davidson

with trees
against sky
& earth grass

dusted upon snow

there are hollow
rusted cars along
the road as though

hungry deer in fields
.

SECOND SEQUENCE: VISIONS

*What did not happen --
brought in ways
that seem to be.*

Ted Enslin

The Holy Ranger

climbs into the
easy chair from
his saddle then
lights his pipe

& removes leather
gloves to hold his
fourteen-month old girl
while the nine-year old

girl tosses soup bones to
Harley the dog whose size
has increased the food budget
this fall & as he gets a kiss
from all these critters he is
still on the ride with Corey
to Butler Biker Days as that

Softail cut trail moving through
traffic like a chrome scout & his
wife hands him a favored Hank Williams, Jr.
album over the baby pulling at white hairs in
his beard: then settling into reveries with
Jim trying to keep the generator trailer
sending power to tattoo needles singing
Fat Bob images or earlier in the week
a wizard chanting on Kelly's arm as
he reaches into a Shovelhead while
out back Doug's trigger job is
explored on the 1911 Model &
then Steve has sold that
Sturgis but only if no
handlebar alteration
takes place when the

Rabbi pulls in on his Full Dresser
which moors at the edge of a photo
taken of Smiley in the Arizona six
gun sun wearing a Derby but by now

Molly has to be in her crib & Sarah
in her bath & me & Maureen might even
meet later on once the house settles into
hallowed silence but for the rasp of exhaust
stutter meditations as The Holy Ranger leans
across a late dinner table reaching for Sunday
night leftovers flavored by a season of roads
taken with comrades chasing mysterious winds   .

The Sportster Accessory

I sure like those Springers
& a Low Rider has always been
my idea of a real motorcycle,

yet this 30th Anniversary Sportster
feels more like a quarter horse for
me with its vibrations instead of bucking:

but one morning I came out to the garage
to find horseshit on the floor & would say
this is quite an official Harley accessory

that research & design got just right
for us who want things rustic & natural --
it's the ideal XLH option

that I'm sure will be
an Eagle Iron catalog
addition with less of   a stink to it but
                       just as much
                       of a pile   .

Memory Inversion

> *The old beast crooks his finger*
> *and the winds start up.*
> *Tonight*
> *it's his only power.*
>   *-- Howard McCord*

1.
hey, baby(which
sounds better during
a guitar break, sure
I know that, you
slink back when
sleep pops open
!today
it is cold, yes
-terday, why
, the sun -- it
was just terrible .

2.
every time
I hit that

spot on the trail
  that spring
leading to the lake
right around dawn I
hear a woodpecker &
rabbits jump out at
the same places .

once I found a snapping
turtle laying eggs too
close to the path &
lifted her out of
the trench & she

28 / Martin Jack Rosenblum

hissed & tried
to hurt me
but I got
her into
cover to
complete
the act.

3.
from here
I can see

the sun moving yet
  across the courtyard
    into bushes
under my window & in my
  office across the sill
    onto a typeface expanding
through inverted
  slats just like
    remembering upon
               .   the office dimmed
                     & there's a need
                      to switch on that
                 lamp I light
                  Virginia flake in
                    a briar instead
          & do not go home, another backlit surface
                 moved upon from
                    another source   .

4.
so that other morning
a turtle is flattened

probably by a car & dried
out it is on the walk in front
of me, timing the final stretch
I ran every day in the fashion
of erupting similarity as with
the hammer on this antique Colt
Pocket Navy clicking into
historical penetration
zones that must synchronize
with those

.

5.
after adjusting the stop-
watch compensating for an

urgent Kung-fu rooting motion
then sweeping kick relieving
this slab from its flat death
onto a trim Lake Drive lawn:

>   as though a burner through
>   my left shoulder in a power
>   drift with free weight rattle
>   syncopation injury back then
>   a healing root sprouted in
>   arcane cells nearer the

warrior blood
which when
spilled
greets dark with dark to have light
                        for this kind
shines into

.

6.
was it yesterday
again, baby (& again
better coming down at
the dominant into minor
riffing to get under more
        when I sliced
        open in kitchen
        psychosis scars
        evidently not
    tempered until
    I crook my whole
    hand deflecting lit porch lamp
    beams starting up into night wind

                .

7.
around dawn seekers muddle back to the stones
& invention will have proven itself or ritual

shall take over   .

8.
mounting the saddle
above chrome V-Twin

Harley-Davidson heads
& turning inserted key
not yet to Sportster light
on position as system wired
capable that way then as initial
gear after sidecut pipes have
produced the familiar rumble
is gotten by leather boot
down on shifter arm
buckhorn bars held:

```
    power has  produced  only  exhaust
    -ing morning idle        which leads
                    to where cobwebs
        still  hang  dew along roadside
         & a stop to warm hands on oil
    tank in hunched reverie
    while pulling the Randall
    from saddlebags to stab a hunk
    of hard bread            inverts
                    memorable use
    so then
    the best
    move is to
    be just warm
    enough to cut
    the bread only


    as feet upon
    hiway pegs next
    pull miles beneath
    for afternoon sun heat
    reflects upon dials  that are measuring how far to go
                    that are lit by unseen bulbs
                along the bezel & when I ease
    into the tall gear & punch Milwaukee Iron
    stones will scatter wasted upon the surface        .
```

Four Wisconsin Photos
Taken from a Harley Pillion Pad

1)   for a distance
          a brick wall
     is in its parts
pieces sorted along
railroad track edges
     to the destination
(more of the purpose
is hidden by that oak.
         there's
a sloppy wooden fence with
a door in it on both sides
the fencing weathered away
one
can
either enter properly
or step through
the fence proper   .

2)   some shopping carts
in a meadow
    black birds on them
four cows pushing
    brush around the siding
an old Plymouth
    the watering bin
other cars perch in directions
    some newer forming
a rusted grid   .

3)   power lines
   hung on vectors
    bridges over
  parallel passages
  the scene goes in
or out it goes seen

        .

4)   snow increases
   its pattern
   binding the landscape
      .look   into
      dark white
   tree branches fallen
              poking out
      shocking grass this
   too a graphic setting .

**Four Wisconsin Photos
Taken from a Harley Pillion Pad**

1)   for a distance
        a brick wall
     is in its parts
pieces sorted along
railroad track edges
     to the destination
(more of the purpose
is hidden by that oak.
         there's
a sloppy wooden fence with
a door in it on both sides
the fencing weathered away
one
can
either enter properly
or step through
the fence proper   .

2)   some shopping carts
in a meadow
    black birds on them
four cows pushing
    brush around the siding
an old Plymouth
    the watering bin
other cars perch in directions
    some newer forming
a rusted grid   .

3)   power lines
   hung on vectors
  bridges over
  parallel passages
  the scene goes in
  or out it goes seen

        .

The Holy Ranger Poems

4)   snow increases
   its pattern
   binding the landscape
      .look   into
      dark white
   tree branches fallen
            poking out
         shocking grass this
   too a graphic setting .

Harley-Davidson
85th Anniversary Homecoming Contemplation

out of the Kenosha holding strip
onto 94 with all areas alongside

covered by raised fists & victory
then on p. 43 of the HD magazine I

find my Harley racing orange front
fender in that photo coming around

the bend in back & my beard sprouting
out from the black helmet -- well being

there in June & here now in my office
between appointments just from buying

this to read & opening my napkin
to keep sandwich crumbs off that

front fender it coming at me
as I was upon it with cycles

behind in columns roaring
& such lovely ladies with

leather fringe sparkling
upon the interstate path

into Milwaukee Iron
coming home I rode:

a pack of Strokers
at my side & front

to rear passion
burning V-Twins

The Holy Ranger Poems / 35

in the mystical
gas tank logos'

signatures   that
chant the poems

I cannot write.

My Photo With a Young Woman

who has a dragon tattoo on her tummy,
is something my dear wife of eighteen
years sees with the knowledge it is a
different kind of chrome for my cycle
& that women are not objects really a
picture like this, man, cannot be taken
away from me as I near my birthday of
forty-two years & anyway with my dear
lady on the pillion pad I cannot find
that photograph especially when there
is a swell in the road & she hangs on

.

The Right Version of the Real War

6,000 U.S. Marines for
77 days held Khe Sanh
while from the Puzzle
Palace all those
Ringknockers told
President Johnson
what he did not want
the six o'clock news
to bring for supper:

that another Dien Bien Phu
could be boiling up from
the Laotian jungle for
which Walter Cronkite
would blame him
so to defoliate
criticism & not

get the proper sight
picture on the NVA's
Dac Cong he arranged
a boondoggle that is

of no use to the Marines
who hold out anyway from

simple anger & an American
interest in proving those
in the field superior to
those who think they are   .

The Holy Ranger as Avenging Angel

for Justice Robert F. P. Schneider --
the only Righteous Hanging Judge left

I. *The Necessity of History*
an American gunfighter is hired by Mormons
who would not protect themselves after
the Civil War & becomes known as an
angel who destroys for those not
inclined to do so

another but also an American gunfighter
        his name never in print
        disappeared into Mexico
        & was more than likely

                the night reflected into
                snow iced over as though
                fears upon the vision an
                instant necessary coming
from a sidestreet looking
through you on a motorcycle
not even seeing this slip as
centered into future's crosshairs

                    :& you cannot open
            fire at the vehicle nearing
        as you are unseen & must wrangle
loose from its incoming blindness not now
as when sighting buffalo running your own
horse down for now we look the collimator
bore-sighting tube in the eye while there
        is yet another incoming object from
        the side ripe from looking at visions
of my father's death last fall(when I got called

I had already dreamed the night before that
I would & this kind of interloping mania of

predisposition magnum disbelief would make
a man's aim steady & choice of pistol only

perfect for the job .

II. *The Restraint of Politics*
somewhere across the border hooves pound
an approach & doves make it damn near illegal
to protect whether one would or not because hawks
of any flight receive legal penalties & if they are
victims their predators have more freedom: because we
are living when an avenging angel suffers not pride but
jury trial & weapons don't work when even a lost gunfighter
cannot ride easily back into proper use & the imagination of
                                          those without help

                                                                    .

III. *The Wisdom of American Origins*
the U.S. Constitution gives me the right
to own firearms of any kind yet I will
not hire out as a gunslinger and due
to an awful demise of courage & ethical sense
       I wonder if that
         destroying angel needs a job
or if the lost outlaw shall
experience resurrection on our
behalf for if we should pull
the trigger lawyers trained
to attack decent motives
feared by cowardice left over from wary
politicians who have eaten too much for
supper will pander us to a legal ambush
unlike those who originated that sacred
American document might ever imagine in
their most worried hearthfire visions of
American determination seen by a common
       eye through iron sights:
that is what Thomas Jefferson spoke for
     us on 19 August 1785:

"A strong body makes the mind strong.
As to the species of exercise, I advise
the gun. While this gives moderate exercise
to the body, it gives boldness, enterprise and
independence to the mind. Games played with
the ball and others of that nature are too
violent for the body and stamp no character on
       the mind. Let your gun
      therefore be the constant
      companion of your walks.
   Never think of taking a book with you."
books says The Holy Ranger are to be taken where

you can park the Harley-Davidson when your
sweetie couldn't make it & the ride needs
hermetic unraveling or even where the
night is falling & she was not there: but
                    on the ghost journey
            indeed that constant companion
            must be a Single-Action in .45
            Long Colt preferably outfitted
            with ivory stocks slung inside
a leather rig worn as well from use as the
binding on a book gets when it is read any
time action needs primer
ideas as ammunition rage   .

IV. *The Possibility of American Resurrection*
we consider death when the most common details
remind us of past experiences with it   .
there are those times too when
the future dies right into
our present preoccupation: here is the time
an Avenging Angel
the last of the gunfighters
dreams a steel & chrome steed upon the land   .

V. *The Harley-Davidson Factor*
it is more than pulling out
the choke & snapping the switch
then turning the petcock & key before
twisting the handle a few times & hitting
the starter button   :
it involves a leg over a saddle to easing
back against the soft embrace of a lady
there in buckskin with fringe falling
slowly over curves that cannot be
found on any road alone
then adjusting that
knife sheath &
hearing a first gear shift that sounds
like the horseshoe on cobblestone near
my father's store where I would head
in the morning before school to wash
the windows & one walk (which was
always taken down the Chicago
& North Western tracks until
I hit Appleton Street in
that the steam engines
made iron horse paths
to follow for a nine
year old Wisconsin
boy lost in Texas
Ranger comics) led me straight into the rasp
              of an elegant Harley fitted
              with a sidehack & ridden
              by a man in black leathers
              who asked me if I needed a
              lift so the rest of the way
              that day I rode to work & never

                         could get out failing my math
                         test & barely passing English
                         I immediately understood what
                         it has taken forty-two years
                         to put into gear -- that
            riding an American Vision is the efficient
                                               revenge for
                   all the cowardice those who deem
             it unfair to defend family with cowpoke
            technology spend upon laws that weaken
            democracy & turn men into snotnosed
            kids needing permission to wipe & ride
                                      away   those
                         who would do us harm

                                       .

VI. *The Courage In That Grace*
handling a Harley around a corner when blacktop
immediately turns to gravel & a foot down won't
save it
gives an
awful strength
to the heart &   your hands can hang on
               to mindful courage all
the time with graceful force & a power
                  rises from history that will not be
                  toppled by fashionable modern laws.

VII. *The Nature of Present Adversity*
there was a time
when a person seen
stealing your horse
would not keep a lawyer
in business for taking
transportation away
was close to murder then

today we see
crimes worse

than horsestealing
pass easily into a

barrister's bargain that
                  time though was
right for you & me & your kids & mine
& your girl & the one to whom I've been
married for nineteen years ,hell ,we have got
                    to listen for the
           hooves pounding as tire
treads rounding
corners of adversity & those not
inclined to be of worthy comradery
                          not
able to stare death down cracking
lips as one cracks the visionary
ground barrier with evolution fury
                          not
willing to take their troubles all
alone when proper with power fire
                    burning into
            unfair practices even if
they are in writing & defense cash

will have to be raised like an
American Flag -- those are not a
bunch to respect so we must hear a

parting of heavenly boundaries
with angelic rumbling & the avenging
holy rider enters our stride & there
comes mystical knowledge chromed for
strength & pride but meaning a

lot more than poetry yet less than
we can say to one another as we
gather around the campfires
hanging onto righteous
sparks that rise into
the night leaving
tracers the eye
alone follows
beyond pages
written by
this light

.

Harley Ownership:
Weekday Morning Rider

leather briefcase
sat upon lawn
  being yanked by
  the woman, removing
weeds flowering (that
my daughter would put
  in a diningroom vase

        .

he waited
as on the
  Harley
I cruised
the alley   .

I could see his glasses
rise when his salutation
   caught me but his return
   to this briefcase & his
woman there on the property
as well pulled a long root
   above the surface

     .

**Upon Finding A Prowler
In The Neighborhood On
The First Warm Morning**

the screen door used
to slap shut in 1959

but the sound of a
deadbolt clunking
into this 1989
doorframe made

>   the night's first
>   summer bugs even
>   fly from the porch
>   light snapped on
>   by a miserable plastic

switch that has taken its place on
the hall wood painted over & much
too layered to strip
            of its protection   .

Mid-Summer on a Harley-Davidson

Wisconsin cornfields strangled without water
& gravel shoulders coughing dust in the wake

of that eighteen-wheeler ahead
so the downshift & then faster

onto this county trunk
as blackbirds' chatter

stick in the windless
hum of tires going to

the broken yellow
lines as a center

for the holy
morning ride

THIRD SEQUENCE: DISTINCTIONS

*What man
goes through to
arrive.*

Cid Corman

History's American Springer

> *"I speak of aesthetic satisfaction.*
> *This want, in America, can only be*
> *filled by knowledge, a poetic knowledge ...."*
>   William Carlos Williams
>   ***In The American Grain***

all the imports hid behind plastic
farings and their riders crouched
on top of them wearing bright
tennis shoes
in the later
eighties when exposed satisfaction
aesthetically sprung onto those
Softail front ends in chromed
        memories of the
        future here in an
        American reply with
        our riders deep inside
        of these machines such
        that every element
        upon Milwaukee
        street poetry was concretely observed through that
                Springer expanding & contracting any
                time the rider's heart would & blood
pulsed through the sparkling coils straight from homemade poetic
                                                                .

In Awe of Friendship

> *Across the tribal brow's hewed ridge.*
> Carl Thayer

the Holy Ranger's buddy
Theodorik woke his wife
one morning in the Maine
light to sing: "hey hey Martin J.!
        how   many   miles   have   ye   rid   today?
        the boys on the bikes is waitin' fer you,
        and so's that girl with the blue tattoo."
the Old Iguana has told tales of the campfires on the low
plains around which steeds were kickstand down & bores are
cleaned & guitars readied for action after seething trail
heat has been dispersed in stories that can be whistled (
in deference to Col. Cooper who asserts memorable poetics
must stay put with traditional meters & who would argue)
: sometimes the riders must
have nicknames to completely
master their feats that day for
these have been such mythological
wonders & on this night the Holy Ranger
was called "Stroker" because he rode with
such passion beyond speed limits accused
of the eleven hundred limit his mount
Ranger possessed so as the Iguana
told it

    .

Theodorik in his boonie hat chopped wood in the Maine sun
that day whistling the rhyme   .

the Old Iguana cranked his Jeep through the Ohio bog with
greater tales for the plains   .

then Stroker walked the wooden steps up to Holy Ranger HQ
in Milwaukee to spin the end   .

       which would not be worth
        much without the friends
such as Kenosha Bandit whose
machine puts these images in
type much the same as having
             been there can
            so when an end
comes riding across the page

it has been on a mysteriously long journey into title awe

Wisconsin Winds

Wisconsin winter crowds the roads
cutting the center line & wrapping
the shoulders
then off into   the fields fenceposts
                stick up as reminders
             of spring's territory
           & the blackbirds upon
          those telephone wires
        call to winter's
attention that
they aren't being scattered by
the holy exhaust roar from the

Harley Sportster that is restrained
by vinyl covering & plastic-coated
chains upon an insulated board in
a garage that is visited late at
night when the house is tight &
the yard flushed by the light
coming from my office window
where the walls are covered
with pictures of motorcycle

Kabbalah: the Old Iguana wearing
            a shoulder rig in the Bog
            the ivory grips like open
            April sunlight
                Willie G. shaking hands
            on a hot June afternoon
               that front mudflap made
            from carriage leather by
            Hunt's Harness on one
            visit to Colgate in
            summer's late heat
                the Holy Ranger
            firing a Buntline Special
            at rogue soda cans along

      the road to the Monches
      dump having dismounted
      to take care of that
      situation before it
      got out of hand
         that Gibson found in a
      sixties ecstasy still
      strung for trouble
      in its hardshell
      battered from
      barroom blues

--these offroad memories found in
frames to contain their snowbound
imagery that develops further an
instant after Wisconsin spring on
the roads cutting about evolution
power drifts like so many friends
in the continuous Midwestern wind

               .

Gibson Guitars On The Old Creek Bed

once I'd selected that
one with the fastest
neck & prettiest
spruce flat-top

I'd head for the ravines
behind my Appleton house

where there was a dried
creek dent in the dirt
& if there upon it
this axe shared
acoustic sustain with a
sparrow then it would go
to the gig : & this selection
                of guitars still
can sing like a bird picking
at the old creek bed   .

They Were
(After Motorcycle Tour)

for Steve Nelson-Raney,
Territorial Rider

a Cardinal
 sits on our
  redwood table
next to the lilacs
 with an abandoned
  Robin's nest
chased away
 they were
  by this
dog who
can ask   to go
out with the smile
of charity   & who

will protect my daughters
with frozen terror that
even Robins cannot live
near in summer daughters

I say as the second shall

come this summer as
Molly Dvora to join
Sarah Terez
& this Cardinal who

will not give up the perch
shared by a mate too & the

dog realizes there is no good
challenge or that their calls

are not for territory just
            for ease of flight
there is peace in the yard

            :the grass simmers
down the cherry tree moves
up &
I am

settling into Zazen
sitting right where

the dog must defecate
so in moving I meditate
in ecstasy with my scooper   .

Harley And The Art Of Motorcycle Magnificence

do not give me any
of that Zen & some

art of motorcycle
maintenance stuff

: just ride your
bike & if it is

not a Harley-Davidson
then maybe you should

just affix it to where
the sun don't rise any

place except through
those rustholes upon

foreign designs stuck
out on American roads

.

The Blues

this gets played in twelve-bar progressions
on my old 12-string with its cherry sunburst
radiating notes that hit the morning sun just
like drops of rain on the backyard grass stepped
upon unmowed & stained where the dog squats to mark
his spot we all later sit with beer cans tucked into
the velvet guitar case which mats the grass like a coffin
would the earth for once we're done all we'll hear is the
blues muffled harking & splitting the night that drops in

.

The Heart Must Beat In An Accurate Hand

for the House Compadres

at fifteen feet or thereabouts
John Wesley Hardin shot playing
cards then autographed them right
before his death dating them in
his last hand -- today we have
General Hatcher's Relative
Stopping Power mathematics
which has sought to gamble
without an ace-in-the-hole
through multiplication of the bullet
weight in pounds times the square of
the velocity and dividing by . . . well

last night a band of us pistoleros left
Greenfield where House of Harley-Davidson
was the fortress from which we rode for Racine
to shoot those nasty bowling pins that created
problems for bowlers all too long & now must
stand before the firing squad & those of us
in the posse who did well were gamblers not
mathematicians (with the exception of yours
truly who is neither mathematician nor any
gambler but who missed those rascal bowling
pins more than not even with that Silvertip
fodder feeding a hungry Colt Combat Elite :
for the art of bringing aim into splintered
wooden bad guys comes from mind to eye with

one's heart as the lens through which
intelligence gets focus & last night
this heart of mine beat to poetic
vision that of course is
material accuracy but still
unsuited for combat measure

                    so   once the cards were shuffled
                    in the kinetic deck with an ace
beneath my fountain pen I imagine a Colt
Single-Action Army in my saddlebags & crank
my Harley against early spring weather
resistance to face objects in absolute

need of control & at fifteen feet the next day
or thereabouts I was dealt an inside
winning hand so I bid on a heart &
raised some & shot
the center right
out of the rusty pot hanging on a fencepost .

Creed

> *Fifty years ago young people were made to understand -around the dinner table- that strife was part of life, and that they might well encounter it, and that it would then be their duty to face it without blinking - ready, willing and able to use force quickly and expertly if necessary. Boys were taught to shoot and use their hands, and girls were taught to expect that in their men.*
> Col. Jeff Cooper
> ***To Ride, Shoot Straight, And Speak The Truth***

the present fear of conflict is producing
reactions that weaken those who would
prefer freedom: if we choose to ride
our motorcycles without helmets
drive our autos without seatbelts   then we
                                         have an
insurance controlled legislature to reckon
with which creates laws that favor our own
best interests whether we like it or not   .

this is not a proper function of my government
& especially since it operates out of scare

we learn that we cannot take care of ourselves
unless it is written that we are doing so well

:the point is not to go without a helmet
                          nor without a seatbelt but
                   to decide without assistance

around the family dinner table
in the absence of television
with the sun's final light
moistening homecooked

meat brought to the
table with a steady aim or
an honest dollar   .

there is a natural order
to all things & the creed
must be to find it beneath
frightful camouflage designed
by those who cannot sense the
power without wanting to take
this from the rest of us now: fifty years ago
                                boys were boys,
                                girls were not,
assistance meant friendship & I mean business.

Pioneers

> *these damn papercollar soldiers*
> Major (Old Gabe) James Bridger

fearing wild beasts
plain & forest
Sarah Terez
sleeps in
the hall with her head through
the doorway to our room   &

Julia on her way to the water
bowl I clear my eyes :
her German Shepherd ears cock
just as a Winchester 94 when
she spots my daughter's nest

then I watch my wife rise
in sleepless splendor
(baby nausea in her flesh

& mine chilled/this winter's edge   ,

                before this day starts
                as light I walk
                  upstairs without
                   a lantern or fire
                   in the hearth
               my Hawken rifle hangs
              with its powder horn
              upon a wall as I hunt
              for a hardbound book
to lay safely

across my lap   .

Physical History

I had a fever during
that deadly spring &
came closer to watch   & stood in
        my backyard one morning
           as Cole Younger rode up

& it is best in a ballad better
yet over a cardgame but he rode

        as the fog lifted & wind
        comes off the lake that
        Bowie slung in a scabbard
        & a carbine on the saddle
I could not
make out which
pistol it was but
I believe he was just
from Texas before hitting
Minnesota & still on decent
terms with the James Brothers

                            but as I
leaned forward just to wipe
mud from my boots he took
the chase & I stumbled
into our fence &
sweating took
off my hat
in disgust   he would
        get caught & I
had to get
        into the clinic
before bleeding more than
could be replenished
from the slugs

left inside
from a
pistol   that went off
           in a genetic outlaw
draw:
an indistinguishable gun held by a   rider that morning
                                       & the Rebel yell
                                       as sunlight
                                       slit by
                    this fir tree when I
                    was brought to my
                    knees then vision
clearing brought summer's bloom
one night as I stood up to hear   my own pulse as a
                                    driven horse into
                                    history's body   .

When There Has Been No Fire

for some time
 it can usually
  be found traced

>   & I consider
>   wagontrails or
>   paths cut by
>   mountain men at

odds with
 wagoneers yet
  ash is the usual

>   distance covered
>   & this can be felt
>   as I shove my hands
>   beneath the leaves &

entirely past
 the waist of
  her slip .

Joining

as when
meeting
it   gets
    this
pioneer/inversion
      which is
      that snow
     upon edge
    , unfrozen
: we never doubt
   it will melt
  nor do we fear
gardens will feed
us serpents any-
        more/than

              keeping loved ones
              together it is the same
              bond that kept the rage

              vicious then a ceremonious
              parting to enhance civilization
              leaving her at the sink & he drove

their old Buick
into the leafpile
while their hall lights
protected the neighbors   .

Air Pirate Disposal Memo

the sign on the U. S. Air jetliner
toilet said: DO NOT THROW FOREIGN
                      OBJECTS IN HERE.
                      THANKYOU.
hell, I had figured that hole
to be a good place to toss
any terrorists on board.
                BUT YOU'RE WELCOME.

Here Goes Proper Country Picking

this Gibson ES-335 resonates through
its cherry top as the Hubbard Park
tunnel flattered my sidecut pipes
& with a slide down the neck
& around a fast curve
hands in gauntlets
& engineer boot
down for one
but just fingerpicks
yet the same boot down
for the other: combine   this Delta beat
                          & that acoustic
                          tunnel rasp for
                  proper country music
                  picking   Milwaukee
                  style when the heart's
                  kickstarter blues goes

                        .

**Enter
(From The Last Autumn Ride)**

the scattered leaves
against the side
of the garage

wet from
an afternoon
rain this fall
the slight wind
in later afternoon
light qualities   :
images receding
from cut edges

into burnt ridges
against a backlit
storm door entry.

**At Milwaukee Chapter
Harley Owners Group
Meetings
We Will**

often marvel
at the chance
meetings & when
one is arranged
possessing   that
element of pure
acausal shock
the intimacy

defines luck   :

as though a tattoo
upon chrome values
tales of the rides
are spun around an
evening's   pleasure
& unwound on roads

where luck
is hardened
not always by
helmets but in
the rush of wind
there are omens of
divine   protection.

Legacy: EvoPoetic Confessional

for Rob Kaleta,
  Caballero

an eagle mind
        an even road will suddenly twist
a wolf heart
        a straight shot can quickly ricochet

:evolution thunder balance
while heading through poetry territorials:

let me admit that my hands
get windburn when I prowl
& cold stiffens them but
win hot lose or draw I
slap leather & hang
onto power that cycles primitive need for the ride
                      which turns & crooks unleashing
                      wild pacts made with tight grip
                      upon buckhorns thrashing as
though wounded in this hunt for significant wind
but if so then healing glove fringe rolls out in
                      the reach for brake levers only
                      when crossroads give hesitation

                                          .

Late Fall on a Harley-Davidson

the leaves scatter into heaps still wet
from night rain & the fog lifts valleys
onto shaded helmet visor visions coming
                            upon a road kill
                as though a ranger
            having followed the trail
        that led to frigid air
impossible to breath quick
so head down right over the stench   .

The Final Draw

The Holy Ranger hits the sack early because he is up at sunrise to ride and then is due back at Holy Ranger Headquarters for steak, eggs and contemplation before the day begins.

This night just before dark he has come from the stable where his steed, *Ranger*, has been wiped down and fed high octane in preparation for the morning trail, and in the distance The Holy Ranger thought he heard riders approaching: but there were none to be seen by the time he reached his back door, so he just went in through the kitchen and grabbed a hunk of hard bread and coffee, lit his favorite pipe as a good omen for the evening's writing, then walked up to his office after lowering The Holy Ranger Flag that flies over Lake Michigan in Milwaukee from Shorewood.

As he eased into his chair to read that morning's poetic meditations for signs to follow this night, he again discerned approaching riders coming up from the ravines along the lake, but when he got up to look out from his room above the treeline there was nothing to be seen but the barn owl from Downer's Woods sitting in the crotch of a tree towering over the flagpole.

He remembered a couple of lines from a poem written long ago: "The owl turns his head from day to night, Never moving his eyes within his turning head." The unrelenting stare of an owl always fascinates, for it reminds us that somebody is always watching -- somebody with knowledge beyond that which we have.

It was soon dark and the only sounds were the ticking of night insects and the rustling of raccoons along the paths out of the woods onto Headquarter property. The following morning, as the cardinals living in the high bushes near the flagpole issued their volleys, The Holy Ranger was uncertain as to whether or not he ever slept; but he decided that perhaps he did, for while the cards were still on the oak table next to his leather chair, the gamblers were nowhere in sight any longer and he did not recall their leavetaking.

He had a clear recollection of their arrival, however, for when Samuel Colt, Orville Gibson, William Harley and the Davidson Brothers climb the stairs to get into a game of five-card stud poker and designate The Holy Ranger as the dealer, leaving their mounts out back to rest after such a hard ride, well, this is a night not easily forgotten. The Holy Ranger dealt hand after hand while he listened to the conversation between his honored guests, and kept a supply of Jack Daniels Old No. 7 on the table for all to increase the warmth of comradery that brisk Wisconsin late October eve.

Samuel Colt was displeased with the ways by which the U.S. Constitution was being weakened to make his invention look bad. He kept shaking his head, swearing that the American form of government was established to protect the common man and woman, and not to make their lives *less* free.

Orville Gibson was not pleased, either, with the situation in 1989. He kept upping the ante, remarking that lewd behavior, strutted behind his invention, made more money for those who had no morals than it did for those who simply handled his design well.

Colt and Gibson agreed that they had no idea their equipment would be abused to such extents, but were pleased their guns and guitars were at least still being made in America.

William S. Harley cut the cards. Arthur Davidson threw chips into the pot, as did Walter and William Davidson. The Holy Ranger dealt from the deck slowly and would often offer his meditations upon the subjects being discussed by his guests. His visions were taken by his elders to mean that he was interested in voicing the ideas that were being brought to the gambling table in a style that was uniquely his own, true, but founded on traditional ideas upheld by innovators outside the territories of literary inspiration.

Harley and the Davidsons agreed that there had to be a revitalization of the Old Ways in this country that produced the rugged individualists of the past, and emphasized that even today it was still possible to Ride Free. Suddenly, the wind picked up outside and we could hear the trees shaking and more leaves falling, and it was time to deal the last hand so these travelers could get back before the Midwestern winter took hold.

It had been a friendly game, though the stakes had been high all along. On the final draw of cards, all players deferred to the dealer to decide the winner of the hand; for while play was by traditional rules assigned to the deck, the cards suddenly were obscured by the ground fog that had risen in the wind off the lake and was blown in through the windows which were open to the pre-dawn fresh air. The room had been filled with smoke and the ashtrays were as full as the bottle was empty.

The Holy Ranger carefully considered each gambler's bid, then cautiously examined as well as he could their individual cards which were on the table for the call.

The sound of the owl could be heard as the day's primary light entered the room. The Holy Ranger was still studying the hands laid around the table when, again, he heard riders; and when he looked up, it dawned on him that his room was as empty as it was the night before his guests arrived.

He felt rested, as though he had a good night's sleep, but there were six groups of five cards laying upon his table and the poker chips were clustered in the center; the morning was coming in and his pipe was out. He got up from his chair to look out the window. The owl, still there, flew away abruptly -- almost as though his watch had ended. Those cardinals fired their waking rounds. There was just enough sunlight rising from the lake to burn off the fog.

The Holy Ranger walked down the wooden stairs from his office to find that his wife and two daughters were still sleeping safely, and that his faithful dog was keeping an eye on the situation so was left in command.
Ranger fired-up immediately, and into the saddlebags went some eats and a flat canteen, and the road along the lake was traveled for some distance before a stop was made to watch the full sunrise: all was quiet in the distance now, as The Holy Ranger, feeling blessed and humbled from the ceremonious night spent at the poker table, realized he saw who had won the game. He looked in his rearview mirrors, the sun ahead causing tears, understanding at last that victory comes to the individual who knows the American past enough to present the future for those who have their gauntlets pulled on, chaps secured and boots on against the bitter years ahead. Out of neutral then into first gear, checking the mirrors to see behind, top gear was reached that morning and held as forward speed was maintained through the first Milwaukee snow shower. The Holy Ranger rode well into that day, returning with sidepipes rumbling in the rhythm of twin cylinders beating as the American pulse is felt by all those who travel this road.

About the Author

Martin Jack Rosenblum has a doctorate in Modern American Poetry and has been affiliated with the University of Wisconsin - Milwaukee for many years, having taught English and presently advising educationally disadvantaged students.

He has published numerous books of poetry and literary philosophy and has edited anthologies of contemporary poetry.

Dr. Rosenblum has a professional standing in the martial arts and is a consultant for a prominent firearms journal.

He has performed as a blues guitarist and toured internationally as a poet and scholar, giving readings from his work and lectures on his research.

He lives with his wife and two daughters in Milwaukee at Holy Ranger Headquarters in Shorewood near the lake.

Selected Books by Martin Jack Rosenblum:

Home (1971)
Brewing: 20 Milwaukee Poets (1972)
The Werewolf Sequence (1974)
as i magic (1976)
Protractive Verse (1976)
Scattered On: Omens & Curses (1976)
Divisions/One (1979)
Brite Shade (1984)
Burning Oak (1986)
Geographics (1986)
Stone Fog (1987)
Conjunction (1987)
Hocket Stutter (1987)
Harley-Davidson Poems (1988)

Selected Audio Tapebooks:

Music Lingo (1987)
Backlit Frontier (1987)